Blooming
in the Dark

Memoirs of a Caregiver

Melissa Babcock Miller

All quotations are from the *New International Bible*, Zondervan Publishing House, 2005.

ISBN: 9798388657503

For permission requests, write to the author at
info@wolfridgefarmhousemarket.com.

 Published by: YesBear Publishing
info@YesBearPublishing.com

~ Contents ~

~ Dedication ~

Josh—

You may have been the one who had to endure cancer and all that it entails, but God used this season to grow me in ways I never could have imagined. I can't wait to see what the future holds for you! I love you, my brave, brave boy.

Stacy –

My husband, father of our children, and my rock of Gibraltar. How could I ever say thank you for all that you are to me? I am still amazed that God brought our lives together and formed our special love story.

Ryan—

You are wise beyond your years. God has gifted you with insight and great love for others. You are my special, miraculous boy.

My Parents—

There are not enough words to express my gratitude for both my parents (Rod and Charlene) and my mother-in-law (Donna) who kept vigil with us during Josh's illness. Now I know that's what parents do.

Mike & Jada—

When a crisis happens, you guys get right to work. Thank you for taking care of all the little things I didn't even think about needing to do. Mike, aka "World's Best Brother" - I can never repay you for being there with Josh when he landed in Houston. Knowing he wasn't alone carried me the last hundred miles to the hospital.

Janet Aikens—

You have been a constant source of encouragement to me
during Josh's treatment and recovery. Thank you for loving
me like you do.

Landa Johnson—

Thank you for your regular reminders to look for what God
was doing . . . even when things were really bad.

~ In Memory of Bonnie Willis Johnson ~

While undergoing cancer treatment herself, Mrs. Bonnie and I enjoyed many hours of fellowship in her living room. Some of that time was spent in Bible study and prayer. Some of that time was spent talking about the lessons God was teaching each of us. In the last few weeks of Mrs. Bonnie's life I was blessed to be able to sit beside her and read chapters from this book. I am eternally grateful for her wisdom, her love, her mentorship, and her friendship.

~ Preface ~

How can you be sure that your faith is real? I've come to learn that real faith is faith that has been tested. It's faith that has met the storms of life and still remained standing when the dawn broke and the destruction was scattered as far as the eye could see. It's not that untested faith is somehow less than; it is simply unproven. The proving ground of my faith arrived in the form of my twenty-one year old son fighting for his life in the midst of an unexpected cancer diagnosis, and I found myself suddenly thrust into terrain that was unfamiliar, intimidating, and terrifying.

As a caregiver, I had a front row seat to some extraordinarily difficult learning opportunities. My eyes were opened, and I was learning that adversity and hardship can strengthen faith and reveal the gaps that need tending. The bedrock of my faith was revealed . . . there were cracks, and some of them were as deep as canyons. It was here that I first realized the gaps between my head knowledge of Christ and my everyday life as a Christ follower. As I dug deeply into the Word and engaged in consistent prayer, those cracks and canyons in my faith began to fill in with God's truth. I began to flourish and bloom, even in this darkest season of my life.

Caregivers face many difficulties, and you will see my honest struggles as you engage with this memoir. I haven't sugarcoated the realities of my experiences; this writing is raw and honest. As you read, it is my hope that God will reveal this truth to you: You can trust God even in the darkest of places or circumstances. You really can grow and bloom in the dark, because God will meet you there, providing examples of His faithfulness through the people you encounter along the way, through the promises of His Word, and through the power of prayer.

Plant your roots in Christ and let him be the foundation for your life. Be strong in your faith, just as you were taught. And be grateful.
Colossians 2:7

Unexpected Sunday Afternoons

September 28, 2018

Friday finally arrived, and little did I know, but it was the beginning of something I never expected: cancer.

My 21-year-old son came home for the weekend with a high fever and chest congestion. The fever clung to him with the tenacity of a bulldog throughout the weekend, and by Sunday morning a trip to urgent care was long overdue. This was no sinus infection, virus, or common cold. Maybe he was having a relapse of pneumonia. After all, he had been diagnosed with walking pneumonia at the end of the summer. By the time we arrived at urgent care, Josh was falling deeply asleep as soon as his body came in contact with a chair. His breathing was shallow and his color was ashy. Still, I held tightly to the belief that his pneumonia had returned. Checking in with the nursing staff at urgent care raised some red flags: his heart rate was over 140, his oxygen level was in the upper 70s, and his temperature was 101 degrees. After a quick look up his nose and down his throat, Josh was sent for a chest x-ray. He returned to the exam room looking more exhausted than ever and promptly fell asleep. Minutes passed by quietly until the PA returned. With a grim look on her face, she asked if I was able to drive him to the local trauma ER or if an ambulance needed to be called. My face must have registered shock, but all of my questions were interrupted by the PA who calmly told me to go to the ER as quickly as I could. She assured me that she had called ahead and that all my questions would be answered there.

Frustrated and unsure of what was going on, I rushed across town to the waiting ER, calling my husband along the way. Now he was on the way to the hospital as well – nearly an hour away. Walking into the ER usually involves checking in and spending what seems like the rest of your life waiting to be called in for triage assessment. Not so today. I approached the desk and gave Josh's name; a wristband was placed on his arm and we were moved immediately to the triage area. You know what comes next: heart rate, blood pressure, temperature, weight. Heart rate . . . 158. Blood pressure . . . high. Temperature . . . 102. Weight . . . no time for that. Josh's heart rate began to increase even more as the triage nurse stepped out to find the doctor. A quick read over Josh's chart prompted the doctor to send him for an emergency CT scan. I find myself being ushered to an exam room with a million questions, yet unable to voice any of them as my son is wheeled away to radiology. What was happening? He just had pneumonia, right? What's a normal heart rate?

Quite a bit of time must have passed. My husband, 15-year-old son, and parents arrived during that time of waiting. Josh, exhausted and frightened, was wheeled back into the exam room. We sit there talking about how Josh has not been himself lately and about how he seems tired all the time. Maybe this really is just a bad case of pneumonia. We've heard that relapses are often worse than the first round of illness. The door opens and the ER doctor enters with a team of nurses and the radiologist. She is very matter of fact. Lymphoma. A very large mass in the chest. The oncologist will be coming by to talk about chemotherapy and radiation. Lymphoma? Chemo? How could that be? Josh had just been diagnosed with walking pneumonia in late July. I still had the x-ray pictures on my phone. Those moments are a blur now, but we must have all begun to rapid fire out questions. We are given the CT results to read:

> Large cystic and solid mass that is arising in the anterior mediastinum and extends into the anterior lower right chest. The mass is extremely large extending from the thoracic inlet to the lung base and measures 17.6 x 10.8 x 8.6cm in size. There is deviation of the cardiac structures to the right and there is a large pericardial effusion. There are bilateral large plural effusions. There is compressive atelectasis without pulmonary nodules or masses. The central airways are maintained. There is compression of the

innominate vein and superior vena cava. There is enhancement of the solid component of the mass. There are no calcifications within the mass. Small nodules in the left anterior mediastinum may represent lymphadenopathy. No supraclavicular or axillary lymphadenopathy. Bony structures of the chest appear unremarkable. Impression: Consider germ cell neoplasm, lymphoma, thymoma, lymphatic malformation.

Lymphoma, according to our doctors, would be treatable and beatable. There are other types of cancer this could be, but they are so rare the doctors don't even want to discuss it with us. People beat lymphoma all the time. It responds quickly to radiation therapy. It really isn't that big of a deal as far as cancer goes.

October 1, 2018

Josh's heart rate goes even higher. He is in pulmonary and cardiac failure. His neck is beginning to swell. We aren't talking about chemo or radiation anymore . . . now the doctors are talking about "life-saving measures". A cardiac surgeon has been called, and Josh must undergo a pericardial window to drain the fluid from his heart. We have no other options. They will try to get a biopsy of the mass during surgery. The surgeon tells us that he may lose him on the table.

By now it seems that the surgery waiting room is full with family and friends. We are all too shocked to speak. Minutes pass by – they seem like eternities. I don't even know if it is morning or night. The world has turned upside down with no warning whatsoever. Finally, we are called to the family conference room. The fluid around Josh's heart was successfully removed, and some tissue from the mass was collected, but there's been an unexpected complication: the fluid that was suffocating Josh's heart had acted as a float for the tumor, keeping it buoyant and safely away from his heart. Without that fluid, the tumor had crashed into his heart, collapsing one chamber and crushing his superior vena cava. I'm no heart surgeon or nurse, so the significance of this news is not fully understood by me. The surgeon explains that the SVC works much like a water hose as it returns the blood from the body back to the heart. Now Josh's cannot work efficiently which will cause strain on his heart and affect the flow of blood throughout his body. Fluid is now building up rapidly in his lungs as well, and his oxygen levels are falling dangerously low. He has been moved to the surgical ICU unit.

Yesterday Josh had a high fever. Today he has oxygen lines, chest tubes, and a surgical incision. He is heavily sedated, and yet his heart rate remains above 150. Even with oxygen administered, his oxygen concentrations are falling.

We remain by his side for hours until the staff tells us we must leave for the night. We find ourselves unable and unwilling to return home, so we check in at a hotel two blocks from the hospital instead. We cannot return to the SICU until visiting hours the next morning. I remember crying. I remember pacing. I remember praying. I don't remember sleeping.

The second day in SICU feels much like the first. Josh is in and out of consciousness and his vitals are unstable. We meet with a radiological oncologist who wants to immediately start radiation therapy. There's still no pathology result, but if this tumor is lymphoma, radiation is our best option. There's only one problem: because of the pressure of the tumor on his heart, Josh can no longer be placed flat on his back, and that's how radiation is administered to the chest. Josh is so unstable that his SICU nurse will need to join him in the ambulance on the ride to the radiation treatment center. That sounds reasonable, but the treatment center is only one block away from the hospital. We begin to question this. If he is that unstable, does he need to be moved at all? Again, staff tells us that we have no other choices. We are looking at a "life-saving measure". It is the middle of the night, and the staff of the oncology center have been called back from their evenings off to try to save our son's life. Oxygen tanks are loaded onto his gurney. The staff has calculated the minutes of oxygen he has and the nurse stands by his side. The ambulance sets out for the treatment, and we set out on foot to the treatment center. Josh's oncologist rigs up a contraption so that he can remain in a seated position during the treatment. He is literally strapped to an office chair and tilted back about 45 degrees. We wait just outside the foot thick lead door that separates us from our son and the dangerous rays of radiation. If only radiation can work, the tumor will begin to shrink immediately giving Josh's heart and lungs much needed relief. The journey is reversed now and we return back to the hospital. Once again, SICU staff sends us away for the night with the promise to call with any changes. We will only be two blocks away. We don't even have a toothbrush. This radiation cycle continues for the next several days. In the midst of treatment, we receive news from the pathology. It isn't lymphoma like the doctors had hoped; it is thymoma. Very rare. Very poor prognosis. The local hospital has never treated this type of cancer.

October 3, 2018

Before dawn my cell phone rings. We are needed at the hospital to sign consent papers to have Josh transferred to MD Anderson for a higher level of care. The staff tells us that he is dying. These are hard words. Hard to hear. Hard to digest. Hard to believe. This is when the waiting begins. Time seems to crawl as we wait for the transfer to MD Anderson. Local hospital staff is working tirelessly to keep Josh comfortable. Our family is able to stay with him in the ICU constantly. We are all praying for a miracle. We wait. And wait. And wait. After almost two full days, we finally have word that a helicopter is approaching to transfer Josh to Houston.

October 4, 2018

This helicopter is staffed with a pilot, EMT, and critical care nurse. Josh will have the same level of care in the air as he has had in the SICU . . . if only. If only he can make it onto the helicopter. Think about the design of a helicopter. They have doors much like a car does, but hospital beds don't fit through those doors; they enter from the rear of the helicopter. If you've ever seen a helicopter up close, you already know that there isn't much room back there. Basically, the doors that allow access to the rear of a helicopter were designed to stow gear. To enter the helicopter would require that Josh be laid flat on his back. This is the one thing SICU doctors have said cannot be done. His heart will stop. His lungs will fail. In a very short period of time. There is no other option. The staff of this specialized helicopter crew come in to prepare Josh for the move. Again, oxygen tanks are checked and rechecked. A plan is in place for entering and exiting the helicopter. Josh's bed begins to be gradually lowered as we approach the helicopter. Now we find ourselves at the belly of the beast. It is time to board the helicopter. The bed is slowly lowered to 30 degrees. It is go time. Josh and the nurses practice the breathing strategy needed to lower the bed flat. It will take a maximum of 15 seconds to get him on the helicopter and back into a 45-degree position. Fifteen seconds. The difference between life and death—this tiny margin of fifteen seconds.

Josh is airborne! We watch as the helicopter banks west and toward Houston. They will be in the air for an hour and a half. Exiting the helicopter will be just as dangerous as entering it.

. . . *Dig into God's Word* . . .

Therefore we do not lose heart. Though outwardly we are wasting away, yet inwardly we are being renewed day by day. For our light and momentary troubles are achieving for us an eternal glory that far outweighs them all. So we fix our eyes not on what is seen, but on what is unseen, since what is seen is temporary, but what is unseen is eternal.

– 2 Corinthians 4:16-18

. . . Think, Pray, Grow . . .

What unexpected troubles are you currently facing that carry a heavy weight?

_____

_____

_____

_____

How can you view these troubles through an eternal lens?

_____

_____

_____

_____

~~Cancer~~

We won't be there; it will take nearly four and a half hours to arrive by car. Four hours is a long time by any standards. It is half of the average American work day. It is longer than a Broadway play. It is longer than a plane ride from Dallas to Los Angeles. It is a terribly long time to think about your son being in an ICU helicopter. My brother, who by the grace of God is a former corporate pilot for the same ambulance service that was transporting Josh, is given clearance to meet the helicopter in Houston. Josh will not be alone. I am so thankful for this. My aching heart was flooded with relief as pictures began to arrive on my phone. Josh was on the ground in Houston and safely out of the helicopter. Those 15 seconds had passed without incident. More pictures come as he is loaded onto a waiting ambulance and rushed to the medical ICU at MD Anderson. My brother stays by his side until we arrive.

Houston is the largest city in Texas. Its skyline can be seen for miles as the highway expands from four lanes into eight lanes. On the last leg of the journey through Houston yet another skyline appears. Locals call it "Medical Center", but it looks like a mini-Houston skyline. Skyscrapers soar overhead as the highway snakes through large urban greenspace parks. The majority of those buildings have "cancer" emblazoned on them. That's when reality struck: my child has cancer.

MD Anderson ~~Cancer~~ Center is our destination. There are several buildings with that name, but we are following signs for the ER and are rapidly approaching the hospital. My sister-in-law meets us in one of the vast lobbies. Those first thirty minutes at the hospital were overwhelming in many ways. The sheer size of the hospital was disorienting. Random seeming lobbies seemed to be the size of our entire hospital at home. It seemed like an unnavigable warren of halls and elevators. I only wanted to see my boy.

Walking into Josh's MICU room was shocking. In the four and a half hours since we saw him lift off from the helipad, he had swollen significantly, and his vital signs had degraded drastically. Before I could even make it to Josh's side, I was stopped by a nurse. Did we have a family history of cancer? How long had he been ill? What was his cancer diagnosis? Did he have a living will? Was he an organ donor? I completely froze. I came face to face with cancer everywhere I turned. Computers screens ~~cancer~~. Staff uniforms – ~~cancer~~. Your son has cancer. *My son* has cancer. *Cancer. He's only 21 years old.* Cancer. It is such an ugly, scary word. Images begin to flood your mind when you hear the word. Those images are followed by every horror story you've ever heard. Cancer – it's a word no one wants to hear.

Only later did I learn the significance of ~~cancer~~. Cancer doesn't have to be a death sentence. But it might be. MD Anderson has covered as many surfaces as possible with the word cancer. But it always looks like this: ~~cancer~~. Why? Because this teaching hospital's goal is to *literally strike out cancer* (Berkowitz). It's funny how a word you dread and fear can lose its power with a simple strikethrough. Suddenly I stopped seeing the word cancer and saw ~~cancer~~ instead.

. . . Dig into God's Word . . .

God is our refuge and strength, an ever-present help in trouble.
Therefore we will not fear, though the earth give way and the
mountains fall into the heart of the sea, though its waters
roar and foam and the mountains quake with their surging.

- Psalm 46:1-3

. . . Think, Pray, Grow . . .

What are you currently facing that cripples you with fear?

_____

_____

_____

_____

Ask God to remove this fear from you and shift your focus to
His providential care for you.

_____

_____

_____

_____

Put Your Lipstick On

Appearances can be so deceiving. In our everyday lives, it is so easy to buy into the deception of appearances. Smiles can be a mask people hide behind; in the same way, frowns can be a barrier that keeps those we encounter at arm's length. Early on after Josh's diagnosis, I found it difficult to "keep my face together". Tears were either flowing down my cheeks or threatening to spill over, and what little makeup I had remaining was far from a priority. How do you maintain appearances in light of a serious diagnosis like cancer? Shock only lasts so long before reality sets in.

I think shock is a good way to describe the first few days of October 2018. After all, Josh had just come home for the weekend with a fever and chest congestion. Cancer was the absolute last thing on my mind on September 29, 2018. By the fourth of October the cold hard truth was beginning to set in. It would be a lie to say that I still wasn't in shock. I was just becoming increasingly aware of how dire the situation really was. Days and nights were a mixed up blur of time spent in the SICU. If you've never found yourself inside a SICU, there are some things you should know: there are no windows, and there is no sense of time. There are only desperate moments that stretch on seemingly endlessly.

As the helicopter that would transport Josh to MD Anderson was inbound to the hospital, my mother sat down beside me and offered some words. Not words of encouragement, but words of wisdom. She quietly took my hand and said, "Put up your hair and fix your face. Josh doesn't need you to fall apart right now. He needs to see his pretty momma with hope in her eyes." She sat there beside me in the SICU waiting room as I robotically pulled my hair up into a bun and smoothed on a little makeup. "That's more like it," she remarked before adding "Now, put on your lipstick and get your game face on."

As I look back on that conversation, I realize now how important appearances can be. I'm not talking about putting on a show to make yourself look better or more important. I'm not advocating that at all. But what I understand now is that my appearance had an impact on everyone around me. It must have been painful for my parents to see me so broken. My then fifteen-year-old must have been frightened out of his mind. My son lying in SICU fighting for his life must have been feeling hopeless. My husband must have been torn between trying to take care of me and standing helplessly at Josh's bedside. And then there's me . . . what about when I stepped into the bathroom only to be greeted by my haggard, tear-stained appearance?

My "game face" started out as just that—a mask that held me together. In the days to come, that made up face and bright red lipstick became my battle armor. Every time that bold red color slid across my lips, it reminded me to put my chin up and trust God's will. That may seem silly and vain, but it is true. That face we look at in the mirror can be our own worst enemy. I know that now. So, if you find yourself fighting an impossible battle, put your lipstick on and face it.

. . . Dig into God's Word . . .

May the God of hope fill you with all joy and peace as you trust in him, so that you may overflow with hope by the power of the Holy Spirit.

- Romans 15:13

. . . Think, Pray, Grow . . .

How can you learn to trust God in the midst of an impossible situation?

_____

_____

_____

_____

Create a "game face" plan to remind yourself to be positive and trust God with the details of your life.

_____

_____

_____

_____

Sabbaticals and Clear Calendars

Maybe you aren't like me. Maybe you wake up each day with a clean slate, eager to see what the day will bring. Not me – I am a planner. My plans have plans. I make lists and mark off the things I accomplish, and, yes, I actually do write down things I do that weren't on my list. And then I mark them off. That's who I am. Or, at least, that's who I used to be. It seems like most of my life has been ordered and very much in control. The truth is that it is all a sham. I wasn't in control of anything. It's the great illusion of life: control. Too many times I relied on my education, training, and expertise. I felt pretty invincible. Nobody got more done than me. I was a wife, a mother, a daughter, a Sunday school teacher, a musician, a high school English teacher, a teacher leader, a district content leader, a fitness coach, a cook, a housekeeper, a quilter, a vacationer, a reader, a photographer, and an artist. I had my world totally under my command.

But I didn't. No matter how hard we try to convince ourselves, we do not have our lives under control. What I hadn't yet learned was what really matters. Was it my family? My career? My hobbies? Some of all of it? One of the first cracks in my fairy tale castle of control was the need to take a sabbatical from my career as a high school English teacher. That meant laying aside much of what I found my identity in: teaching. I don't think any one of us sets out to let our careers step in front of our families, but, if we are honest, it just seems to happen. Grading papers every night and weekend instead of helping your kids study, reading for classes instead of reading your kids a bedtime story . . . well, you get the picture. It is a slippery slope. I wanted to be respected for my work as a teacher and up and coming educational leader in my district, but it was coming at the expense of my family.

My son's cancer diagnosis cleared my calendar. It deleted my lists. Oftentimes people talk about what cancer can't do, but what cancer can do is set your priorities in order. Suddenly my clean house and graded papers didn't have much significance. I didn't care so much about how I was dressed or what people thought of me. I wasn't worried about that presentation on Wednesday anymore.

What I started to take a closer look at was my real priority: being a Christ follower. At the time of Josh's diagnosis, I had been teaching a ladies Sunday school class at my church for more than a year. So many times I would teach about what it meant to have real faith, what it meant to trust God's will when we don't understand it, what it means to "put feet to our faith". All those things are easy to say, but when we face the real trials of life, they aren't so easy to do. I found myself praying more than ever. My simple prayer was something like this: "God, I don't understand, but I trust You." I prayed that over and over again. I studied my Bible with a hunger I have never had before. My greatest desire was to know God's heart. I thought about God in His mercy sending His only Son to die on the cross for the sins of humanity. What kind of love is that? Not one I can wrap my mind around. I read prophesies of Jesus from the Old Testament where the prophets said it "pleased God" to crush Him. I returned to Proverbs to study my favorite verses about not leaning on your own understanding. I settled on James 5:16 - "the prayer of a righteous person is powerful and effective." I poured over that single verse in all the Bible versions I could get my hands on. I did word studies based on that verse. What I learned was prayer is powerful. Prayer is effective. Prayer that comes from the heart of the righteous cannot be thwarted. That's when I changed the focus of my prayers. I started praying for a clean heart before God. I asked Him to make His priorities my priorities.

. . . Dig into God's Word . . .

Create in me a pure heart, O God, and renew a steadfast spirit within me.

- Romans 15:13

. . . Think, Pray, Grow . . .

What do you need to confess to God so that you will have a clean heart before Him?

_____

_____

_____

What are some of God's priorities that need to become your priorities?

_____

_____

_____

Write a prayer asking God to shift your priorities into sync with His.

_____

_____

_____

Everybody Is Here for the Same Reason

Have you ever had a moment when you realize that something isn't about you? My husband and I sat down for lunch in the MD Anderson cafeteria which has a seating capacity of nearly 1,000 guests. My sweet husband (who is usually the Rock of Gibraltar) looked across the table from me and said, "You know what's really sad? All these people are here for the same reason." Just a quiet observation, but that's the moment when I realized Josh's cancer diagnosis wasn't about us or even about our story. Here we were in the largest hospital complex *in the world.* How could we use this unique platform? How could we stop looking at our own circumstances? How could we find purpose in this crisis? When we are able to shift our focus away from ourselves, that's when we can truly reach out to others. We are all doing life together whether we like it or not. I was literally sitting with nearly 1,000 people who knew *exactly* what I was going through.

In those moments of clarity, I understood that even though my life at present was unbelievably difficult, the same was true of the people around me. I looked across the cafeteria and saw people young and old from every corner of the globe. Heaven will be just like that, but without the sickness and pain that we endure here on earth. It is so easy to slip into self-pity and wallow in it, but seasons of distress must drive us to show mercy and compassion to others. This season of heartbreak and pain wasn't about me; it was about learning how to reach out to others.

Engage people—hear their stories. Offer five minutes of your precious time to let someone tell you what's on their heart. Share a hug with a grieving wife you meet in the family room. Pray with a total stranger. Teach an elderly person how to use their cell phone to manage appointments. Share the source of your hope with the people in your elevator car.

Jesus calls His followers to be the "salt" and "light "of the world. When we finally realize that we-all of humanity-are here for the same reason, we will find ourselves more than willing to do just that. We are all trying to survive this thing called life. Even in the midst of our deepest pain, we must reach out to others and share the only hope we have – Jesus Christ.

. . . Dig into God's Word . . .

You are the salt of the earth. But if the salt loses its saltiness, how can it be made salty again? It is no longer good for anything, except to be thrown out and trampled underfoot. You are the light of the world. A town built on a hill cannot be hidden. Neither do people light a lamp and put it under a bowl. Instead they put it on its stand, and it gives light to everyone in the house. In the same way, let your light shine before others, that they may see your good deeds and glorify your Father in heaven.

- Matthew 5:13-16

. . . Think, Pray, Grow . . .

How willing are you to share the Good News of Jesus with others?

_____

_____

_____

_____

Write a prayer asking God to increase your willingness to share the gospel with others.

_____

_____

_____

_____

Heavy Metals

I have never been much of a fan of heavy metal music. I lived through the 80s as a teenager, and even then, I still wasn't a fan. Those screeching guitars, the screaming voices, the endless riffs . . . not a pleasing sound to my ears. Josh's chemotherapy largely consisted of heavy metals (Drugs: How Chemotherapy Works); the backbone of his chemo regimen was cisplatin. Does that name remind you of anything? It should: platinum. That's right, my son's chemo pumped his body full of platinum, one of nature's heaviest metals. Those treatments didn't come with screeching guitars, screaming voices, and endless riffs, but they did come with profuse sweating, bed-shaking chills, and vomit of volcanic proportions. Needless to say, I enjoyed these heavy metals even less than the heavy metal of the 80s.

Our lives often get heavy metals pumped into them too: disappointments, broken relationships, illnesses, and shattered dreams. Life is uncertain and difficult. Once you come to terms with that fact, you can begin to do something about the heavy metals in your life. Just like a cancer patient must consume water to counteract the effects of chemotherapy, you must seek relief from the heavy metals that come into your life. It is so easy to slip into the mentality that the circumstances of life are unfair or too hard, but this is where faith must be coupled with action. Seek God's will in the midst of your disappointments. Use the Bible as a guide for mending broken relationships, and accept the fact that restoration isn't always possible. Use your illness as a platform to minister to others who are fighting similar battles. Sweep away the fragments of your broken dreams and then pray for wisdom as you form new dreams.

God has promised His children that He will use all things for our good. Consider the life of Joseph. His brothers hated him because he was their father's most favored child. They despised the content of his dreams. They plotted against him, considered taking his life, and ultimately sold him into slavery. Joseph rose to prominence in the household of Potiphar whose wife accused him of rape when he refused her advances. Potiphar, who previously trusted Joseph with his entire household, had him thrown into prison. In prison Joseph rose yet again to prominence as an interpreter of dreams. His gift catapulted him to an audience before Pharaoh himself. Joseph's godly wisdom was noted by Pharaoh, and as a result, Joseph became the most important person in the kingdom beside Pharaoh himself. As Pharaoh's second in command, Joseph finally understood the promise

God had made to him when he told his starving brothers that what they meant for harm, God meant for good.

The same is true for you: what seems in your life to be meant for your destruction, God can use for your good. That doesn't mean that your life will be perfect or problem-free; in fact, life can be very painful and messy. But in the midst of those heavy metal times, seek God's face. Ask Him to show you how He is using this difficulty to draw you closer to Himself, and He will.

... Dig into God's Word ...

And we know that in all things God works for the good of those who love him, who have been called according to his purpose.

- Romans 8:28

... Think, Pray, Grow ...

In what areas of your life do you need to seek God's face?

_____

_____

_____

_____

Write a prayer asking God to help you seek His will. Ask Him to give you confidence in His care for you.

_____

_____

_____

_____

Nobel Prizes and Parades

Dr. Jim Alison is the first scientist from MD Anderson to ever be awarded the Nobel Prize in Physiology and Medicine (Merville). His stunning achievement "identified and discovered how to unleash a brake on the immune system." This research is at the heart of cutting-edge immunotherapy treatments that are saving the lives of cancer patients all over the world. Friday, October 5, 2018, marked a day of celebration at MD Anderson with a parade in Dr. Alison's honor. Crowds lined the sky bridge, halls, and lobbies to give a Texas-sized shout out to Dr. Alison's work. I want to be sure you get this image right, so let me elaborate: a marching band, banners, signs, shouting groupies, paparazzi, and security – all inside the hospital.

I don't want in any way to minimize the significance of Dr. Alison's work. It is astounding and worthy of this recognition; however, I'd like to put it into the timeline of our journey through Josh's cancer. This great celebration happened the day after we arrived at MD Anderson, just a few days after Josh's horrifying diagnosis. I had just been run out of the medical ICU while Josh was having his first PICC line inserted, and this was the scene that welcomed me when I stepped off the elevator in one of the lobbies. Well, this really was not my finest hour. I'm sure the hostility could be easily read in my face. I wanted to make all the noise stop. I wanted that band to stop playing its happy little march. I wanted to scream at the top of my lungs for people to see my pain. I also had absolutely no idea what was going on. I had never heard of Dr. Jim Alison and knew little (ok, nothing) about immunotherapy. I didn't know that the whole hospital was celebrating something remarkable that gave many people newfound hope for recovery.

As I took a seat with my family, I noticed that they were all very excited about this parade. Someone passed me a cup of coffee and excitedly talked about the doctor, the research, and the Nobel Prize. My mom put her arm around me and said, "Just think . . . this doctor, his research . . . it might be part of Josh's treatment." Talk about getting the chair kicked out from under you! There I was having a pity party (ok, a little tantrum) and my mom was swept up in the excitement of the *possibility* of a cure. That would be the first of many moments in this journey where I was ill-equipped to understand what was right in front of me.

There are some important lessons I learned from that day. As time moved away from those first days at MD Anderson, I found myself a bit curious about Dr. Jim Alison and his research. The hospital was covered with banners announcing his award. Eventually, I read some articles about Dr. Alison, his research, and immunotherapy in general. The more I read, the more I became convinced that God is working in ways I can't comprehend. I will be the first to admit that I don't understand immunology, but the more I learned, the more I praised God for His infinite wisdom. I very quickly moved away from my little pity party to celebrating the way God had revealed this knowledge to Dr. Alison. I also learned the power that comes from celebrating others' joy. Now that I thought back on that parade, I was able to celebrate (albeit a bit late) with those staff members, patients, and families who were overflowing with joy because this research could improve the quality of life and survival rates for many people suffering from cancer. I started looking for evidence of immunotherapy and engaging those patients by speaking of the great joy of that celebration and praying with them that God would use this therapy to give them comfort, relief, and healing. Ultimately, this episode taught me to grab every spark of hope. Once I had a better understanding of the significance of that parade, it sparked hope in me. I would catch myself rereading those banners each time I passed them, because they were a reminder of the ongoing cause to defeat cancer. The conversations that were born from what I learned were not only hope building in me, but they also built hope in others. That's what happens when we latch on to the sparks of hope that come our way.

. . . Dig into God's Word . . .

Now faith is the assurance of things hoped for, the conviction of things not seen.

- Hebrews 11:1

Let us hold fast to the confession of our hope without wavering; for He who promised is faithful.

- Hebrews 10:23

A cheerful heart is good medicine, but a crushed spirit dries up the bones.

- Proverbs 17:22

. . . Think, Pray, Grow . . .

Reflect on a time that God worked in ways you didn't understand during a season of difficulty in your life.

_____

_____

_____

How does considering God's faithfulness to you remind you to have hope in God?

_____

_____

_____

Dressing Room Disasters

PTSD is a real thing. Soldiers go to war and are forever left with the scars of the horrors they've encountered on the battlefield. What you might not hear much about, though, is the struggles faced by caregivers. Caregivers' worlds are just as radically changed as the worlds of their patients. Just like someone facing a serious illness, caregivers must often abandon their careers, families, and normal routines to care for their loved ones. Emerging research is taking a closer look at the long-term health effects of caregivers, and health care providers are supporting caregivers as they battle alongside patients in ways they never have before (Support for Caregivers of Cancer Patients).

Entering back into "normal" life can be challenging for caregivers. For me, doing so-called normal things during my son's cancer treatment was quite challenging. Attempting to pick up a pair of jeans and a sweatshirt ended with crying in the dressing room for half an hour. Walking into a grocery store was overwhelming. Driving a few blocks in my car was coupled with endless calculating of how far I was from the hospital. I couldn't enjoy a meal without looking at my watch a dozen times to see how long I had been gone. It seemed that everywhere I went, people were blindly and blissfully moving through their "normal" lives while my son was a few miles away fighting for his life.

Fast forward to "normal" life after that patient is on the road to recovery. Everything looks promising, yet caregivers can find themselves crippled by fear. What if someone with flu comes to visit? What if he passes out in the shower while I'm home alone with him? What if his fever spikes? What if, what if? This is where the connection between PTSD and the stress caregivers face is much the same. Soldiers returning from war are in no actual danger, but their brains can't seem to shut off fear. They often relive moments of terror that are triggered by the simplest sights, smells, and sounds. In the same way, caregivers' minds are overflowing with what to look for, medication schedules, and a gnawing fear that lurks around every corner. On this flip side of illness, it seems only reasonable that caregivers should be able to rest and relax, knowing the hardest part of the journey is behind, but fear is not rational.

Fear comes the moment our eyes shift away from the solid rock of faith. Consider Peter's story: When Jesus called him to walk on the water, he responded in obedience. He stepped out of the boat and literally began to walk on the water toward his master. But when Peter looked around at the crashing waves, he was crippled by his fear and began to sink. Matthew 14:30-32 records what happened:

> *But when he [Peter] saw the wind, he was afraid, and beginning to sink he cried out, "Lord, save me." Jesus immediately reached out his hand and took hold of him, saying to him, "O you of little faith, why did you doubt?" And when they got into the boat, the wind ceased.*

If you find yourself looking at the size of the crashing waves in your life, do what Peter did. Cry out to Jesus for help. He will immediately grab your hand and pull you to Himself. Maybe the storms of your life won't subside as quickly as they did in Peter's case, but as long as you hold on to Jesus, the storms won't matter.

. . . Dig into God's Word . . .

From the ends of the earth I call to you, I call as my heart grows faint; lead me to the rock that is higher than I.

- Psalm 61:2

. . . Think, Pray, Grow . . .

What are some "waves" that are crashing into your life right now?

_____

_____

_____

_____

Write a prayer asking Jesus to draw you close to Himself and to focus your attention on Him, and to protect you in the midst of this storm.

_____

_____

_____

_____

Put It in Your Right Ear

Being the caregiver for someone facing a serious illness takes a toll on you. You find yourself physically and mentally exhausted for weeks on end. You move like a robot. You eat like a hungry wolf so you can get back in the hospital room. You sleep in fragmented snatches. Until . . . until an anchor comes along to hold you steady for a moment.

One of my anchors was my then fifteen-year-old son Ryan. Night after night, he would crawl up in the bed beside me and pass me one of his headphones. Every single night he would have to say, "Put it in your right ear, Mom" as I fumbled with the earpiece. He would offer me a song of encouragement before I tried to sleep. He played songs by his favorite Christian band while we laid there with our heads together and tears in our eyes. One song he played often for me was "Tomorrow" by Unspoken (*Lyrics*). These are the lyrics of the chorus:

> *Don't know what tomorrow holds*
> *I'm learning how to let it go*
> *Jesus, You are in control*
> *Of my tomorrow . . .*

Come and take the fear away
'Til there's nothing left but faith
I know You will help me face
My tomorrow . . .

Those moments spent by my fifteen-year-old's side were a literal shelter for my spirit. When the day was done at the hospital, and my husband and I had switched shifts for the night, I needed these times of refreshing more than I could have possibly known. While I had spent the day being a caregiver for Josh, Ryan had spent the day searching out the just right song to minister to his mom.

Being an anchor in times of trouble requires more than happenstance. It takes intentionality. Jesus doesn't just "happen to be" the anchor for our souls. God intentionally planned for Jesus to offer Himself as a sacrifice for sinful mankind. Jesus is in control of our todays and tomorrows. He alone can remove fear and replace it with faith.

. . . Dig into God's Word . . .

Have I not commanded you? Be strong and courageous. Do not be afraid; do not be discouraged, for the Lord your God will be with you wherever you go.

- Joshua 1:9

. . . Think, Pray, Grow . . .

How can focusing on the sovereignty of God become an anchor for your spirit?

_____

_____

_____

_____

Write a prayer asking God to shelter your spirit.

_____

_____

_____

_____

Crazy Socks and Caramel Corn

Some days are easier than others. When you, or someone you love, is battling a serious illness, this is especially true. In the beginning of the battle with a long term illness, there are so many friends and family members standing helplessly around waiting and hospital rooms. Then, as days turn into weeks or even months, that crowd begins to dwindle. I think it is important here to talk about some of the whys.

Reason #1: life goes on. Life goes on for the immediate family and closest friends. Bills must be paid, therefore, someone must go to work. Yards still need mowing, and animals still need feeding. Our family found itself in this same position. My husband needed to return to work so that our insurance wouldn't lapse and our household bills would be paid. Our youngest son needed to return to his classes in public school. My parents needed to return home to care for themselves and their small farm. Extended family had their own lives to return to. Friends could only visit after work hours. It isn't that you don't understand the necessity of almost everyone returning to their lives, it is just a very lonely time. Sick people sleep for hours. Caregivers have hours of time on their hands to think and wonder, and usually that's done in dark rooms in the middle of the day. Nighttime sleep is fractured by the around-the-clock nature of life in the hospital. You find yourself sleeping in minutes instead of hours, eating meals like a starved wolf, and bleary eyed from hours of television or reading. Life goes on while it seems that life has come to a dramatic halt for the patient and left-behind caregiver. After the first whirlwind of days, Josh and I found ourselves spending almost every minute of every day together. That brings me to reason #2 . . .

Reason #2: patients need a little space. When that waiting room crowd drops down to one, patients need space. Being with the same person around the clock for weeks in a row gets a little tricky. How many ways can I tell you to take a sip of water? How many times do you need me to help you into the bathroom? How many movies can we watch? What do you want to eat? When are you going to get out of that bed and walk around the unit? And the questions go on and on until someone snaps. I'd like to say that Josh was the one to snap first, but that just isn't true. It was me. Mom. I'm supposed to be the grown up in the room, but Josh's constant refusal to get out of bed pushed me past my breaking point. In a self-righteous huff, I cornered up the nurse and angrily told her my frustrations. Dealing with Josh was like dealing with a five-year-old. He refused to get out of bed. He refused to drink anything. He refused to order any lunch. I was quickly losing my patience. I really expected our nurse to take my side in this; after all, all the things I was pressing Josh to do were exactly the things she was telling him to do. Much to my surprise, our nurse asked me if I had any cash. I was completely dumbfounded. Was I going to start bribing him with money to do these things? Certainly not! Our nurse stood quietly by my side as I dug through my backpack looking for money. I found a $100 bill, and she said, "that'll work just fine." Still clueless, I turned to her with money in hand, awaiting my orders. She sent me shopping. Seriously. She asked me to go down to the gift shop and buy Josh some crazy socks. She also asked me to try some of the caramel corn. She literally sent me packing. As it turns out, that little venture out of the room was exactly the space Josh and I both desperately needed. I returned to the room to a happy camper who was drinking a soda and excited about those socks. I had munched on the most delicious caramel corn I have ever tasted and had a better attitude. We both needed that reset.

How often do we find ourselves in similar positions? The trials and heartaches of our own lives are often faced alone. It seems that the rest of the world is going on with their happy little lives while we are caught in the midst of the fight of our life. It can be lonely. It can be isolating. It can be overwhelming. It can feel like the walls are closing in. But, the truth is, none of us is facing anything that someone else hasn't already faced or is in the midst of right now. We desperately need one another. That's how God designed us to live: in relationships with one another. What if we faced our own trials by reaching out to others who are on the backside of the same kind of storm? What if we pulled alongside someone who is facing the same thing we are? Could that help? Absolutely. When we join together with other believers to work through the challenges of life, something beautiful happens. We find ourselves exactly where God wants us to be. We live life together just like we saw in the early days of the New Testament church. Don't miss the power of this kind of living; the world sees it, and it is radically different.

. . . Dig into God's Word . . .

By this everyone will know that you are my disciples, if you love one another.

- John 13:35

. . . Think, Pray, Grow . . .

Reflect on a time you felt alone in the midst of a trial.

_____

_____

_____

_____

Write a prayer asking God to grow your relationships so that you can be strengthened and so that you can strengthen others who are facing trials.

_____

_____

_____

_____

Isolation

In a hospital setting isolation is a clinical term. It involves intentionally separating a patient with a compromised immune system from outside contact for the purpose of preserving the patient's health. The patient cannot come in contact with another human being unless there are gowns, masks, and gloves separating them. Medical staff know that this separation is detrimental to a patient's overall well-being (Abad et al.).

Unfortunately, the same thing too often happens in our day to day lives. We find ourselves in seasons of isolation. These seasons of isolation often accompany the times in our lives when we are the most vulnerable and spiritually sick. Sometimes we are too quickly convinced that separating ourselves from others is the best course of action. You may stop attending your small group Bible study, resign from a role of leadership, or stop responding to messages from your friends and family. You might still be attending church with your heart and mind closed off to those around you, and that's isolation, too. It doesn't really matter what your isolation looks like; it is the attitude of your heart that matters most. Pulling away from others can be helpful and necessary during seasons of your life, but that cannot be your normal state.

In the parable of the vine, Jesus taught that believers must remain rooted in Him. Without that connection, we wither and die. The same is true of our lives within the family of believers. When we isolate ourselves from fellowship, prayer, and Bible study, we begin to wither spiritually. Imagine that shoot from a grapevine that got accidentally clipped by the weed eater. It is dead already, but it doesn't even know it. It doesn't really matter what your isolation looks like; whatever the cause or reason, force yourself to get reconnected.

. . . Dig into God's Word . . .

"I am the true vine, and my Father is the gardener. He cuts off every branch in me that bears no fruit, while every branch that does bear fruit he prunes so that it will be even more fruitful. You are already clean because of the work I have spoken to you. Remain in me, as I also remain in you. No branch can bear fruit by itself; it must remain in the vine. Neither can you bear fruit unless you remain in me. "I am the vine; you are the branches. If you remain in me and I in you, you will bear much fruit; apart from me you can do nothing. If you do not remain in me, you are like a branch that is thrown away and withers; such branches are picked up, thrown in the fire and burned. If you remain in me and my words remain in you, ask whatever you wish, and it will be done for you. This is to my Father's glory, that you bear much fruit, showing yourselves to be my disciples."

- John 15:1-8

. . . Think, Pray, Grow . . .

How can staying "rooted" in your faith family strengthen you?

_____

_____

_____

Reflect on a time you isolated yourself from others. Ask God to strengthen your relationships with your faith family.

_____

_____

Haircuts That Hurt

Chemotherapy is awful. If you've never experienced it for yourself or watched someone you love endure it, you have no idea of how terrible it can be. It seems like it is one of those cases where the cure is worse than the disease. Imagine having your body pumped full of chemicals that work like atomic bombs, killing everything – good and bad – that they encounter. Imagine sitting in the dark watching that constant drip at 2 AM. It's terrifying.

Most cancer patients lose their hair at some point during treatments, and it was just a matter of time before Josh's hair began to fall out. At first there were a few stray hairs on his pillow. Next there were clumps of hair on his pillow. Then we were using lint rollers to try to keep up with the falling hair. Finally, there was the hair clogging up the shower drain. I'm talking about handfuls of hair that completely covered the drain. By this time, Josh's sheets were being changed two to three times a day just to keep up with the loose hair. That's when his nurses told us the time had come to cut his hair. Either they could do it, or it would be my job. Since I had always been the one to cut Josh's hair, he wanted me to do it.

This is a good time for a confession . . . I think I approached this haircut with Pinterest stars in my eyes. I somehow convinced myself that I could turn this haircut into a cutesy little process. I tried to cut his hair into a "faux hawk" and then into a Mohawk. By the time I started the Mohawk, it was clear that just cutting it off was the best option. I started by combing what remained which just left bald patches in the wake of the comb. Finally, I laid the comb down and used the clippers to closely shave what was left. And Josh was practically bald. That's when the tears started. He was devastated, and I struggled to understand why. In a practical sense, cutting his hair was necessary and made him more comfortable. On an emotional level, it was the proverbial straw that broke the camel's back. He stood hairless in the bathroom searching his reflection. He choked out, "I have cancer." It was a haircut that hurt.

It's easy to hide behind the illusion of health or prosperity. As long as everything looks ok, you tend to buy into the lie. Maybe what you really need is a haircut that hurts. What is it that God needs to strip away to show you just how helpless you are without Him?

...Dig into God's Word...

In the same way, the Spirit helps us in our weakness. We do not know what we ought to pray for, but the Spirit himself intercedes for us through wordless groans. And he who searches our hearts knows the mind of the Spirit, because the Spirit intercedes for God's people in accordance with the will of God.

- Romans 8:26-27

...Think, Pray, Grow...

Reflect on a time God stripped away something in your life that revealed your helplessness.

_____

_____

_____

_____

Write a prayer asking God to strip away anything that has decreased your dependence on Him.

_____

_____

_____

_____

World Travelers . . . Sort of

"Be careful what you wish for" is a familiar saying. Since early childhood, Josh has had an insatiable thirst for travel. I suppose I helped fuel that thirst by teaching him to research vacations in advance. We would learn about geography and culture long before reaching our destination. By the age of ten he had been to nearly every state in the continental US, and after high school graduation our family spent two weeks in the Canadian Rockies. He spent many hours learning about other cultures; Egypt and Rome especially fascinated him. He's one of those nerdy kids DuoLingo was created for . . . he thought learning to read Greek would be a good investment for his time. He learned to speak Spanish and was quite the little expert on Egyptian hieroglyphics. We often talked about traveling to Italy when he graduated from college.

During the first days and weeks at MD Anderson, Josh found himself surrounded by people from every corner of the globe: his nurses were from Sudan, the Philippines, and India; his doctors were from China and Switzerland; one of his respiratory therapists was from Egypt; and our food service waitress was from Jamaica. During the many hours of chemotherapy, I watched as my son engaged this varied slice of humanity. I saw that tiny spark of curiosity as he asked people where they were originally from. I watched as he engaged people from all over the world. And I started thinking about how often we feel defeated because our dreams don't become reality. Josh was, at that particular time, facing a very uncertain future. He wasn't responding to chemotherapy, and his strength was fading as his body tried to fight cancer. It would have been so easy for him to fall back in that hospital bed and give up on his dream of traveling the world, but that's not what he did. Instead, he let his dream change. He let the world come to him. He took advantage of those encounters with people from places he may never go. He learned about others' customs and what they loved about their home countries.

What about us? Are we willing to let our dreams change? Or do we just let our dreams wither up and die when it seems like hope is lost? As children we are quick to set our hearts on dreams that are often far beyond our reach, but as adults we are quick to abandon those dreams before we even attempt to reach them. It seems like we live life being a little too "careful what we wish for". The same is true for our walk with Christ. We intend to serve in the local church, to go on a mission trip, to share our faith with everyone we encounter. The first time we face any obstacle, though, we too often find those dreams and intentions quietly fading away. Rejection from others causes us to shy away from sharing the gospel. Criticism leads to church servants' resignations. Schedules keep us from participating in mission work. One day of skipping Bible reading turns into weeks without studying God's word.

What would it take for us to be willing to lay aside our hopes and dreams in order to serve Christ the way He intends? He calls us to share the good news of the gospel *as we go* through our daily lives. He demands that we take up our cross and follow Him. He commands us to love others as He loves us. Dream big . . . how will God use you to draw the world to Himself?

... Dig into God's Word ...

"Therefore go and make disciples of all nations, baptizing them in the name of the Father and of the Son and of the Holy Spirit, and teaching them to obey everything I have commanded you. And surely I am with you always, to the very end of the age."

- Matthew 28:19-20

... Think, Pray, Grow ...

What are some obstacles that have caused you to abandon God's mission?

_____

_____

_____

_____

Write a prayer asking God to use you to draw others to Himself.

_____

_____

_____

_____

Letting Go

After my nephew was born, our family learned that he had a rare chromosomal deletion. At birth, he was deaf, vision impaired, free bleeding, and physically deformed. My sister-in-law and brother were devastated. The pregnancy had been typical and worry free. They had no idea that their precious baby boy would be born with this litany of medical concerns. Doctors said he would never live to leave the hospital, but he did. Doctors said he would never ride in a normal car seat, but he did. Doctors said he would never walk, but he did. Doctors said he would never be able to speak or hear, but he does. Doctors said he would never be able to eat normally, but refried beans are his favorite food. Doctors said he would never be able to learn, but he is a clever eleven-year-old. It is all these "buts" that need a little more attention. Although my nephew is able to do all these things doctors said he would never accomplish, he doesn't do them all in conventional ways. At seven, he still rode in a toddler's car seat because of his small stature. He learned to walk with the help of countless hours of physical and occupational therapy. He hears with the aid of a cochlear implant. He speaks through sign language. He eats, but only pureed foods. He attends public school but takes special classes to help him learn. Our entire family had to learn how to "let go" of the all the normal things we expected. And it was painful. All the dreams that we held for him weren't necessarily attainable in the way we hoped. Watching my nephew grow and develop in his own time and on his own terms has been remarkable. My sister-in-law and brother would say that they had to mourn the things that would never be. They had to wipe the future clean of the plans they had in order to accept the plans God had for their collective future.

In much the same way, my son's cancer diagnosis came with the need to "let go" of the plans we had for his life. After living on his own for more than three years, he needed to move back home. He had to withdraw from his university studies so that he could take treatments. He lost his love for playing piano. His memory failed. His attention span disappeared. Instead of being a vibrant 21-year-old, he spent most days in his pajamas listlessly watching old episodes of NCIS. This change was even more difficult for me than enduring hours of treatment and uncertainty. In the midst of his treatments and surgery, my hope was always just to get through it. I was so laser-focused on preserving his life that I gave no thought whatsoever to life after cancer. As it turns out, life after cancer is just as challenging. Yes, Josh's cancer was gone completely, but the hard work seemed to be just beginning. Physical barriers like fatigue, dizziness, and nausea were still daily battles. Emotional barriers like loneliness, depression, and isolation were stronger than ever. Mental barriers like memory, reasoning, and thinking proved to be the toughest to tackle. In many ways Josh was much like a young child trapped in his adult body.

While my husband and I were busy making plans for Josh to return to life as normal, his body, mind, and spirit were putting the brakes on with all their might. Once again we found ourselves and our plans put on hold. It was during those times that I often reflected on the birth of my nephew and how obvious his lifelong struggles would be from that moment on. I thought about how when my own son was born, he was perfect in my eyes. Now I know that the cells that caused his cancer were already present in his tiny little six pound, fourteen ounce body on August 9, 1997 (*Mediastinal*). For twenty-one years we lived under that umbrella of deception. We bought into his seemingly perfect health and bright future. Now, reality slapped us in the face. Our plans simply no longer existed. More than ever, we placed our faith in God and His sovereign will. God allowed cancer and all of its repercussions into Josh's life for a reason. We just needed to "let go" of our plans so that we could seek His.

. . . Dig into God's Word . . .

"For I know the plans I have for you," declares the Lord, "plans to prosper you and not to harm you, plans to give you hope and a future."

- Jeremiah 29:11

Why, you do not even know what will happen tomorrow. What is your life? You are a mist that appears for a little while and then vanishes. Instead, you ought to say, "If it is the Lord's will, we will live and do his or that."

- James 4:14-15

. . . Think, Pray, Grow . . .

What are your "perfect" plans that have met roadblocks or setbacks?

_____

_____

_____

_____

Write a prayer asking God to help you "let go" of your plans so that you can seek His will.

_____

_____

_____

_____

Wrong Turns and Chemo Fog

It is a scientific fact that people undergoing chemotherapy experience something called "chemo fog" (Chemo brain). According to the Mayo Clinic, the term describes thinking and memory problems that can occur during or after cancer treatment. Symptoms can include confusion, difficulty concentrating, difficulty finding the right word, mental fogginess, short attention span, and fatigue. All these symptoms are expected and understandable . . . for the patient.

What about for caregivers? Do they experience the same disorienting symptoms? Well, I certainly did. During one of our brief stays at home, I needed to drive toward my brother's house in south Louisiana. I have made that trip hundreds of times, yet I found myself at a red light turning the wrong direction. I'm not talking about missing a turn in town. I'm talking about taking a turn to the wrong town. Instead of heading east, I was heading west. Toward the other end of the state. And I didn't even know it. Thankfully my mom was in the car and quietly asked where I was headed.

Realizing I wasn't in full control of my thinking was a bit shocking to me. I thought I had everything under control. I had my calendar and my medical notebook. I never travelled anywhere without my "go bag". What I had failed to realize is that I wasn't quite as mentally prepared as I believed I was. I was going through life on a sort of autopilot with my mind a couple of hundred miles down the road.

As I reflect on 2 Corinthians 10:5 which says, "we take captive every thought to make it obedient to Christ," I realize how dangerous it is to go through life without being in control of our thoughts. Too often, we let our minds aimlessly wander or focus on the wrong things. We forget to stay focused on Christ and His will for our lives. We sit through Sunday school with our minds on a million other things. We catch ourselves wondering if we turned the crockpot on before heading out the door for church. We fall asleep during our personal Bible study time. All these wanderings are dangerous. The Bible teaches us that our enemy roams about seeking ones to "devour". Like the cartoons of our childhood, we will be too quick to let the wolf in when we aren't aware of our thoughts. Instead, we must intentionally set our minds on the right things.

... Dig into God's Word ...

Finally, brothers and sisters, whatever is true, whatever is noble, whatever is right, whatever is pure, whatever is lovely, whatever is admirable—if anything is excellent or praiseworthy—think about such things.

- Philippians 4:8

... Think, Pray, Grow ...

Reflect on a time when you allowed your thoughts to be out of control. What damage did it cause?

_____

_____

_____

_____

Write a prayer to God asking Him to direct your thoughts and protect your mind.

_____

_____

_____

_____

Hotel Living

Not many things excite me more than a vacation. I love to travel and especially love to check into a hotel for the night. There's something very liberating about not having to make the bed, clean the toilets, or vacuum the floor. (Maybe you need to be a mom to appreciate that!) During Josh's treatments we spent weeks at a time in a hotel near the hospital. Let me just say that the luster wore off quickly. You know you've been living in the hotel too long when you know all the staff by name, know which washing machine takes your money, and know which dryer shrinks your clothes. No matter how hard I tried, I couldn't convert that hotel room into home. It wasn't just the physical space that was different, it was the absence of family that made the space unbearable. Even when my husband and I were both in the same town and the same time, we never had the same schedule. Our only interactions were much the same as shift workers at shift change. We used our notebooks to review the day and passed one another like ships in the night. Seldom were we able to eat a meal together or sleep in the same bed.

Each time Josh was discharged from the hospital but needing to remain nearby, the two of us settled into the hotel for a week or so. I would light a candle, toss his fleece blanket across the sofa, turn on the tv, open the curtains, and cook in the kitchenette. All of these vain attempts to make that hotel room "homey" were miserable failures. We still weren't home, and we were still separated from our family. What we longed for was home--home where we belonged. In the weeks after Josh's treatment, I finally started to see the bigger picture. We spend so much time in this lifetime making our homes into perfect retreats filled with the treasures of a life well lived, but we never seem fully satisfied. That's because these homes we work so hard to perfect are not our real homes. God has placed eternity in our hearts, and we won't feel truly home until we are found in the presence of our Savior in Heaven.

. . . Dig into God's Word . . .

But our citizenship is in heaven. And we eagerly await a Savior from there, the Lord Jesus Christ.

- Philippians 3:20

But in keeping with his promise we are looking forward to a new heaven and a new earth, where righteousness dwells.

- 2 Peter 3:13

. . . Think, Pray, Grow . . .

Reflect on your life and home. Are you more focused on creating a perfect "nest" than you are investing in things that last for eternity? What things or priorities reveal your true focus?

_____

_____

_____

_____

Write a prayer asking God to shift your focus toward eternity.

_____

_____

_____

_____

'Tis but a Scratch

Chemo was finally finished and it was time for surgery to remove the final parts of Josh's tumor. Even though I was more than ready to get that thing out of his chest, I was horrified at the thought of what the surgery entailed. His surgery would be open sternum which meant his chest would be cut open, separating his breastbone and ribs to create access to his heart. I just couldn't let my mind go there, so I simply focused on the part I wanted to think about—getting rid of that tumor. After surgery, Josh spent several days with a wound vac. We called it our piglet because it made little oinking sounds around the clock. This device is meant to aid in healing by keeping the incision area dry and sterile. All we could see was a strip of purple foam tape covered by a clear gelatin-like patch that ran down the center of his chest. Days later (and at home, no less) we would be able to see the incision for the first time.

That open sternum surgery was extensive, with much more to it than the removal of a tumor. The lining of Josh's heart was removed and replaced with gortex. A portion of his bronchial veins was removed. A section of his right lung was resected. Had I known beforehand, I would have been paralyzed with fear at all the things that could go wrong. Now that I knew what his surgery entailed, I had built up his incision site to epic proportions in my mind. Imagine my surprise upon seeing Josh's surgical scar . . . it was hardly a scratch! What I had built up in mind didn't exist at all. I'm ashamed to say this, but these were familiar waters for me. Too many times in my life I've blown things out of proportion, created terrifying scenarios in my mind, and stressed out over things that never came to be. I'm pretty sure that I'm not alone in this. It's the human condition to wonder and worry. How many times do we have to go through that same process before we learn that "each day has enough trouble of its own"?

When you spend your time consumed with the "what ifs" of tomorrow, you shift the focus of your faith from God to yourself. When I think back to those days surrounding Josh's surgery, I realize that I wasted quite a bit of time worrying about things I couldn't control instead of giving them over to the One who already has control. Maybe you need to join me in praying for God's help in laying down the reins of control in your life. Perhaps it is time to remember that God is God, and you are not.

. . . Dig into God's Word . . .

Draw near to God, and He will draw near to you. Cleanse your hands, you sinners, and purify your hearts, you double-minded.

- James 4:8

Therefore do not worry about tomorrow, for tomorrow will worry about itself. Each day has enough trouble of its own.

- Matthew 6:34

. . . Think, Pray, Grow . . .

Reflect on a time when you were consumed with "what ifs" that distracted you from God's faithfulness.

_____

_____

_____

_____

Write a prayer in which you give a specific "trouble" or "what if" to God. Ask Him to help you trust Him more.

_____

_____

_____

_____

Victory Laps

Nearly a month had passed since Josh's surgery, and it was time to take our first victory lap. Since the beginning of our journey, we had kept in contact with one of our SICU nurses from Rapides Hospital. Randy, our former nurse, was instrumental in organizing a visit back to the SICU, and many of the nurses and doctors who were working during our brief stay were there for the reunion. I had prepared an obscenely large basket of snacks and sodas for the staff . . . after all, I am from the South where we celebrate everything with food. How do you thank the staff who saved your child's life? I knew my gift was nothing more than a trinket in comparison to the gift they had given me. The ride to the hospital was tense. Josh spoke little and kept his head down for the entirety of the ride. As we approached the hospital, he finally spoke up. The truth was that he had absolutely no memory of having even been in this hospital. When I reminded him of his nurse and doctor's names, he didn't remember that either. He didn't remember the ambulance rides to the radiation unit, and he didn't remember the helicopter ride to MD Anderson. He was becoming more and more anxious with every block. Not knowing what else to do,

I continued on to the hospital. The staff who were waiting for our arrival would have likely understood if we hadn't shown up, but I felt we simply must go. We entered the hospital, and Josh became agitated and asked to leave. As I look back on this day, I realize now that this was the day I first became aware of the extent of Josh's memory gaps. I valiantly tried to convince myself that he had just been too sick at the time to log it in his memory.

This was the day we had been waiting for and nothing was going as I had imagined. In my mind, a victory lap was going to be a joyous experience. We would jump around, hug, and high five. In reality, I walked my sullen and withdrawn son up to the SICU with a heavy heart. My heart was racing with unbelief at his lack of memory. My mind was filled with images of the days spent in this hospital. My feet slowed as we neared the final door to the SICU. It seemed like that last door weighed so much more than I remembered. Finally we arrived at the security buzzer, and I pressed the call button and asked for Randy. Within seconds the doors opened and out walked the familiar faces of the staff who had cared for us. I stood somewhat awkwardly to the side as they all flocked to Josh much as a group of ladies would to a newborn baby. They touched his arms, face, and head. One nurse raised his shirt to look at the scars on his back from radiation burns. Another pulled down the neck of his shirt to look at his chest scar. One stood quietly weeping in the corner. Randy repeatedly hugged Josh while saying, "It's a miracle. It's a miracle." In the midst of that flurry of activity, Josh stood silent and still at its core. When the staff finally made a little space around him, he simply said, "I'm sorry, but I don't remember you." No one on the staff seemed shocked by this; in fact, many of them assured him that it didn't matter because they remembered him. By now the staff was beginning to turn its attention to me. They reminded me to take care of my own health, to be patient with the recovery process, to take Josh to all of his follow-up appointments, to feed him healthy food, and to make him rest. One nurse took me to the side and said, "When something bad happens in my life, I'm going to call you. You must have some special connection to God, because your son shouldn't be alive right now."

I've often reflected on the things the SICU staff said to me that day. Most of it was common sense (even if it bears repeating). But that final statement is the one that keeps returning to the forefront of my mind. I had started that journey to the hospital for the purpose of celebrating Josh's victory over cancer, but God was showing me His victory over sin, death, and Hell. Even this likely unbelieving nurse recognized the power of God in this situation. Her comment opened the door for me to share my faith with her. She had seen me at the lowest point in my life, yet she had seen more than my pain. She had seen my faith. I spoke openly with her about my trust in Christ for my salvation and how that lead me to trust Him with everything else, too. I was honest about how difficult Josh's illness was and about how heart-broken I was, but I was also honest about the deep-seated peace I felt in the midst of that storm because of my faith in God and His will.

It seems like that day really was a victory lap . . . we just weren't celebrating what I had expected. That got me thinking: how often do we celebrate the milestones of life with an intensity that far outweighs the celebration of the working of Christ in our lives? We will cheer for our favorite sports team, sit for hours in the sun to watch a Little League game, plan birthday parties for months in advance, talk endlessly about our hobbies or vacation plans, but will remain silent about Christ. Even when opportunities to speak truth and life to people present themselves, we tend to stick to "safe" subjects. This has to change, because we need to take our commission seriously. Christ has called us to make disciples of all nations. Aside from loving God with all our heart, mind, and soul, this is our one job. How will we stand before God and account for our lack of enthusiasm in worship, our lack of obedience in evangelism, and our lack of discipleship in people's lives?

. . . Dig into God's Word . . .

But in your hearts revere Christ as Lord. Always be prepared to give an answer to everyone who asks you to give the reason for the hope that you have. But do this with gentleness and respect.

- 1 Peter 3:15

. . . Think, Pray, Grow . . .

Evaluate how you spend a typical day. Then, be honest with yourself . . . How much of your day is spent pursuing your will and how much is spent pursuing God's will?

_____

_____

_____

_____

Write a prayer asking God to reset your priorities until they align with His will and His Word.

_____

_____

_____

_____

Geez, Mom!

"Why do you make every little thing such a big deal?" I
get this question lately from Josh more often than I'd care to
admit. Pardon me, but I get excited when I see forward
progress. Got an "A" on your speech . . . started working on
campus as a tutor . . . got yourself out of bed without my help
. . . haven't needed a nap in a week . . . Well, let's just say
that I'd like to shout these accomplishments from the roof.
Why? Because I've finally learned an important truth: every
moment is a "big deal". Unfortunately, I had to learn this
lesson the hard way; but that doesn't mean you have to learn
it that way.

How do we learn to live each moment to its fullest
potential? That's what Shakespeare would call the "rub" or
the big dilemma. I think we would first have to make some
hard decisions about what fully living each moment entails.
Is it pleasurable experiences? Times of great happiness?
Contentment? Financial security? Good health? Serving
others? Ultimately, fully living must be defined by our core
values. What we value is what we will seek, and finding what
we seek is how we measure life. One of the things that I have
come to value during this chapter of my life is the power of

seeing the "God moments" in the everyday. When I seek to understand how God is working in the here and now, it changes how I view my day. I start to look at my day as the gift that God intended it to be in my life. I start to look for ways to serve Him and others. I start to see His fingerprints in the smallest details of my life, and that's certainly a "big deal".

Another way to define living each moment to its fullest potential is by learning what it is not. It's not days marked by fear, bitterness, and discouragement. It's not spent with a spirit of doubt and unforgiveness. It's not moments wasted focused on the past and its regrets. It's not anguishing over the perfect opportunity before making a move. Learning to make the most of life's moments means living a life firmly rooted in Christ. When you begin to look at life through His eyes, you'll find much to celebrate! You can replace your fear with hope when you look to Christ and know that He "will help you" and uphold you with His "righteous right hand" (Isaiah 41:10). You can be strong and courageous when you know God "will not leave you or forsake you" (Deuteronomy 31:6).You can extend forgiveness to others because Christ extended forgiveness to you. You can put your disappointments and discouragements behind you when you learn that God's "grace is sufficient" (2 Corinthians 12:9). You can stop waiting for the perfect opportunities and instead wait on God.

This is what living each moment to its fullest potential looks like—seeking God first.

. . . Dig into God's Word . . .

But seek first the kingdom of God and his righteousness, and all these things will be added to you.

— Matthew 6:33

. . . Think, Pray, Grow . . .

Make a list of things in your life that are keeping you from living a life of godly potential.

_____

_____

_____

_____

Write a prayer which confesses to God the things in your life that keep you from living up to your godly potential. Ask God to help you seek Him first in all you do.

_____

_____

_____

_____

Soul CT Scans

CT scans, MRIs, and x-rays are noninvasive methods medical professionals use to look beneath the surface of the human body. These scans can reveal diseases and abnormalities with stunning efficiency. Whenever Josh undergoes a CT scan of his brain to monitor any spread of cancer, our family jokes that his doctors are just making sure he still has a brain. In all seriousness, these scans are pretty nerve wracking for me. It was a CT scan that first gave us the diagnosis of cancer, so I always find myself a little apprehensive when it is time for another one. It seems like I hold my breath until I see those clear scans and read the radiology report for myself. Sitting around waiting for those results makes me reflect on how little we know about our own bodies.

Psalm 139:14 says that we can praise God because we are "fearfully and wonderfully made." I would be the first to admit that I am marveled by the human body. Think of all the tiny little cells that work together in a functioning organ, the synapses in nerves that send signals across the body, or the way the brain stores and retrieves memories. It is mind-boggling to say the least and gives us pause as we think about the greatness of God. Not only did He create us to function in this marvelous fashion, He is also intimately knowledgeable of our innermost being. He knows our thoughts and intentions.

If only we could look beneath the surface of our lives and see what lies deep inside us – in our hearts and minds. Jeremiah 17:9 teaches that the heart of a person is desperately wicked. How many times do we bury that wickedness behind a fake smile or a kind act? How much of what we do each day is for our own benefit? It has been often said that we can fool people most of the time, but we can never fool God. He sees us for who we really are – and He loves us still. We can call out to God like David did, asking God to exam and test our minds and hearts. When we ask God to perform these "soul CT scans", we can be assured that He will reveal our sin to us. Invite God to study your heart and mind, then listen to His report as He points out the things that displease Him. Then, just as you would begin a course of medical action if cancer was discovered, begin the journey of repentance. It won't be easy, and it probably won't be comfortable, but it is necessary.

. . . Dig into God's Word . . .

The heart is more deceitful than all else and is desperately sick; who can understand it?

- Jeremiah 17:9

Examine me, O Lord, and try me; Test my mind and my heart.

- Psalm 26:2

. . . Think, Pray, Grow . . .

Reflect on some ways your life is out of sync with God. Where are there discrepancies in how you think, feel, and act?

_____

_____

_____

_____

Write a prayer asking God to examine your heart and reveal anything that displeases Him.

_____

_____

_____

_____

I'm Hungry and Other Answered Prayers

Have you ever given much thought to what you eat in a day? Not the calories, fat, or sugar counts . . . just the process of eating. One of the lingering issues in Josh's recovery has been the mechanics of eating. Radiation burns led to strictures in the throat which reduced Josh's ability to swallow. At first solid foods were tolerable, but then eating his beloved chicken strips became more than he could bear. Soon afterward drinking the shakes we were relying on for calories became impossible. Almost immediately the ability to drink water was gone. Hours without nutrition turned into days without consuming anything more than a painful sip or two. When Josh's weight began to plummet, liquid nutrition via IV became necessary. Until that day I had not given much thought toward the mechanics of eating. It would be fair to say that I had taken the act itself for granted. Even now, many months after treatment is complete and cancer has left his body, eating continues to be a struggle. Not every day, mind you, but more often than not. The number of meals that I have cooked that have gone uneaten by Josh is staggering. The bottles of Gatorade reserved for Josh never seem to get depleted, and a pantry full of snacks remains uneaten.

Part of me knows that this is yet another long term effect of cancer treatment, but I often find myself begging him to eat. (It would be fair to say here that begging isn't the right word – a better substitute would likely be demanding.) This simple act of eating a meal has proven to be one of our greatest challenges. How can he expect to regain his strength without eating? How can his weight recover without eating? How can he get his body functioning normally without eating?

I wish I could say that after all we have faced through this journey that I would be quick to pray first instead of trying everything in my power to fix the situation. But, alas, that would be a lie. Instead of praying and asking God to intervene in this situation, I just cooked. And cooked. And cooked. I have tried it all – home cooking, pizza, cookies, Thai, ice cream, and everything in between. I have purchased every kind of Gatorade, drink flavor, soda, and juice. Most of it all went into the garbage. Oh, there's such a powerful message there: the things we do in our own strength are about as worthless as garbage.

Imagine my surprise as I drove home from yet another trip to the grocery store -- where I had walked miles seeking that elusive thing he would eat or drink – and heard the chorus of Matthew West's song "Strong Enough" on the radio:

> I know I'm not strong enough to be
> Everything that I'm supposed to be
> I give up
> I'm not strong enough
>
> Hands of mercy won't you cover me
> Lord right now I'm asking you to be
> Strong enough
> Strong enough
> For the both of us
>
> (Matthew West Lyrics).

It was as if I could hear God asking me how long I was going to try to fix this myself. After all the battles He had fought for me, here I was again in the uncomfortable place of being confronted with my self-reliance. As I sat parked on the side of the road, I was broken by my sin. Yes, sin. Any time we find ourselves working apart from God, that's sin. In those moments, I was reminded of my study into the power of prayer –and I started praying right then. Within seconds my cell phone rang, and it was one of my prayer partners. She simply said that God had overwhelmed her with the need to call me *right then*. Tears flooded my face as I told her what I was doing and how desperately I needed Josh to eat. She began to pray with me over the phone, and I was moved by the simplicity of her prayer. She said, "God, make Josh hungry." That night, nothing happened. I threw away yet another untouched dinner plate. But . . . the next morning was something altogether amazing.

When Josh woke up that next day, his first words were, "Mom, I'm *hungry.*" He ate that day like the starved man that he was . . . he didn't just eat a little breakfast, he ate plates of it! Watching him eat that day was the specific answer to specific prayers. Talk about empowering! Think of all the wasted energy, money, and frustration I had spent trying to solve this problem in my own strength. Compare all that waste with how quickly God righted that situation when I released my control and my prayer partner was obedient to the Holy Spirit's urging.

. . . *Dig into God's Word* . . .

Do not be anxious about anything, but in every situation, by prayer and petition, with thanksgiving, present your requests to God.

- Philippians 4:6

. . . Think, Pray, Grow . . .

What have you done in your on strength that ended up being "garbage"?

_____

_____

_____

_____

Write a prayer thanking God for answering a specific prayer.

_____

_____

_____

Write a reminder to yourself about what it means to release control and trust God instead.

_____

_____

_____

_____

Pity and Well Wishes

If you're interested in what really drives me to the point of no return, I will tell you: pity and well wishes. One of the things I've learned about myself during this season with Josh's cancer and recovery is that I just do not handle people's sympathy well. There's something about the way a person's entire demeanor and voice change when the "C word" comes up. Suddenly the person you were just chatting with physically draws away, almost as if cancer was contagious. Now that same person is speaking to you in a mournful whisper. Next, the hand patting begins. And, finally, the empty well wishes . . . "everything happens for a reason", "God won't place more on you than you can bear", "everything is going to be just fine", and "I'll be thinking about you".

Maybe you are familiar with this kind of sympathy, but I hope you are not. That's because the sympathy I'm describing feels incredibly phony to the recipient. It feels like hogwash. Let's examine the scene a bit closer:

The Physical Drawback: When someone shares their struggles and trials with another human being, the response should be to lean in, not to lean away. Unfortunately, the physical drawback is the typical response. A psychologist would probably label this as a defense mechanism. Life is hard, and everyone has problems. The truth is, we all need one another. We need the support of our families, friends, and neighbors as we walk through dark valleys. We need the support of strangers we meet in doctor's offices and checkout lines. Christ calls us to bear one another's burdens. How can we do that if we lean away from those who share their burdens with us?

The Mournful Whisper: When a person shares his or her story of brokenness, respond to them in the same way they spoke to you. If it started out a whispered conversation, feel free to keep it that way. Otherwise, don't assume the funeral parlor volume. You know what I'm talking about . . . soft-spoken whispers tinged with the sound of sorrow. Often times when people share their heartache they are looking for support and encouragement, not for agreement with the severity of the problem. Trust me, I know how dark my situation is, and I'm looking for someone to shed a little light on it.

The Hand Patting: I don't need you to pat my hand. I need you to hold it! Patting my hand just makes me feel even more helpless than I already did. But when you hold my hand, I feel like I have someone else in my corner. Someone who will stand by my side. Someone who will pick me up when I am down. Truthfully, this is what every person needs. As we face the struggles of life, we each need someone to have a hold on us. When we realize that we are "forever family" with our brothers and sisters in Christ, this connection will become more automatic. While you're holding that hand, remind that brokenhearted person that more than anything, they must hold onto the hand of God.

The Empty Well Wishes: Thank you very much, but I am well aware that "everything happens for a reason." I know those verses about everything working out for good, but the truth is, I just don't want to hear it right now. Why? Because my heart is broken. Because my world has been flipped upside down. Because I can't yet see how God will work this out for my good. You say, "God won't place more on you than you can bear." I know that's nowhere close to the truth. I can't bear this at all. All I have is my dependence on the character of God. He loved me enough to send Christ to redeem me even while I was still a sinner. He loves me enough to preserve my faith in the midst of this. His word reminds me to cast my cares on Him instead of on myself. Now you say "everything is going to be just fine" . . . well, can you personally guarantee that? I didn't think so. Finally you say, "I'll be thinking about you". Will you? Really? Don't say it if you don't mean it. So what do you say? You honestly and lovingly say, "I'm sorry you are having to face this." And you leave it at that. It isn't the time for empty words or promises you can't deliver. You don't ask "What can I do?" You just do something. Anything. Bring a cup of coffee or a meal or sit beside the grief stricken for thirty minutes without saying anything at all.

. . . Dig into God's Word . . .

"My command is this: Love each other as I have loved you."

- John 15:12

Bear one another's burdens, and so fulfill the law of Christ.

- Galatians 6:2

Two are better than one, because they have a good return for their labor: If either of them falls down, one can help the other up. But pity anyone who falls and has no one to help them up..

- Ecclesiastes 4:9-10

"Fear not, for I am with you; be not dismayed, for I am your God. I will strengthen you, yes, I will help you, I will uphold you with My righteous right hand."

- Isaiah 41:10

. . . Think, Pray, Grow . . .

What are some tangible ways you can show Christ's love to someone walking through a life-storm?

_____

_____

_____

Write a prayer asking God to use you to show His love to someone who is hurting.

_____

_____

I Just Want To Stay in Bed Today

Life can be hard, brutal even. Sometimes it is hard to get out of bed in the morning because the weight of your day feels like a two ton truck on your chest. So, you'd rather just stay in bed today. It will perhaps be less painful than the reality that awaits you on the other side of your warm covers. Don't pretend you don't know what I'm talking about, because we've all been there. Afraid to take that first step of the day, you just want to sink a little deeper into that mattress. That's where I've found my son too many times. He can be overwhelmed and derailed by the smallest setbacks, and his immediate response is to hide in his bed. This is heartbreaking to watch because I see so much to be thankful for. I see where God has brought him from, and my heart is full of joy. I still see that dark valley of cancer in my rearview mirror and it gives me perspective. But on those days he just wants to stay in bed, I feel like I am on an uphill journey without traction. I get frustrated. I get angry. I get discouraged. But then the momma bear in me kicks into high gear . . .

I try to get Josh to see the little accomplishments that he's made and how they are adding up to something incredible. I remind him of where he was a short while ago and point out where he is right now. I honestly say that I really don't know how he is feeling. I tell him that I am proud of him because he keeps fighting. I tell him that I love him. I remind him the things that I can see God doing in his life. I remind him that God isn't finished with him yet. And then I tell him to get out of bed and face the day.

Some say that when you stop moving, you're dead. That's how I view those days when it would be easier to just stay in bed. It might feel like a necessary rest, but, in reality, it is a trap. You can't give in and sink into the quicksand of despair. You must try to keep moving forward. Perhaps you need to connect with a support group, seek counseling with your pastor, or consult with your medical team . . . all of those things are steps forward.

You're right: you can't handle this day alone. Each day is a choice. You can choose to look to God and let His strength renew you, giving you the strength you need. Or, you can keep hiding under your covers, trying to figure everything out on your own. Whatever fears you have are no surprise to God, yet he asks you to "cast all your anxiety on the Lord because He cares for you" (I Peter 5:7). You can trust God with your eternal salvation, so can't you trust Him for today too?

. . . Dig into God's Word . . .

For the spirit God gave us does not make us timid, but gives us power, love and self-discipline.

- 2 Timothy 1:7

. . . Think, Pray, Grow . . .

When have you been tempted to give up?

_____

_____

_____

_____

Write a prayer asking God to renew your strength so that you can face the day ahead.

_____

_____

_____

_____

One Year Later

September 30, 2019, is our first "cancerversary". It is one year to the day from Josh's cancer diagnosis. So much has changed in his life and in our family. It is a somber day—one in which we reflect on where we've been and where we've yet to go. It's a day of thankfulness, but it is also a day of heartbreak. A year later and the shock of it all is still fresh. A year later and cancer is behind us. A year later and recovery is still many miles away.

Time is a tricky thing . . . a year can seem like it flies by, or it can seem like it drags on for an eternity; and, sometimes, a year can feel frustratingly slow and dizzyingly fast at the same time. Some say that time heals all wounds, but no one ever says how long that time takes. In the world we live in today, time is seen as our most precious resource. How do we decide how to spend this resource? The truth is that sometimes we get to decide, and sometimes we don't. Perhaps you have some master timeline for your life. You've set benchmarks for personal goals, but you suddenly find yourself on a detour. The path you had set out on is no longer clear or moving on the timeline you've established. Not only are you on a detour, but you're also on one that is unfamiliar and unmarked—you have no idea where this detour will take you, and you are unsure of how long this new path will take— and, let's be honest: it's a scary place to be.

As I reflect back on this past year, I am filled with gratitude. I try to remain positive. I try to embrace the "new normal" of our lives. I think about how much I have changed in the last year, and how I view life differently now. But I am also often consumed with worry. I slip into negative thoughts. I become fearful of every sniffle and headache. I think I still try to pretend that somehow everything will be "normal" again. It seems like this year has brought about some positive things in my life, but it still hasn't fully released me from some deeply seated negative things. I've definitely been on a detour, and I still can't see the end.

These past three hundred and sixty-five days have been the hardest of my life, but they have also been the most fulfilling. That may seem an odd thing to say in light of my son having cancer, but I firmly believe that in our hardest days we can grow the most. It is in the darkest night, the toughest battle, the most raging storm that we come face to face with the most critical question: Is Jesus enough? For me, this past year has solidified my response to this question with a resounding "YES". On the slow days and the fast days, it was my faith in Christ that gave me strength to put one foot in front of the other. Christ has drawn me closer to

Himself than I could have ever imagined.

These are a few of the lessons I have learned along the way:

- *Just when you think everything is going perfectly in your life . . . you'll find out it isn't.* Anything can happen. You or someone you love could be diagnosed with a serious illness, you could be seriously injured in a car accident, you could lose your job, your marriage or family could fall apart, etc., etc.

- *You aren't the only one with problems.* Seriously. All you have to do is look around and make yourself available to others to see that every person on the planet is facing a struggle. Your problems and struggles may not look like mine, but they are just as serious to you as mine are to me. When we start to realize that we aren't the only ones suffering, we can truly begin to lean on others for support while we simultaneously reach out to support others.

- *Yes, you can.* Whatever you are walking through, whatever you are facing, you can face it. Can you face it alone? Not at all. Will it work out the way you hope? Not necessarily. But there is a way to survive it. Turn to Christ and let Him carry you. Read His word and discover that He is enough.

- *Two steps forward, ten steps back.* Don't be caught off guard when good days go bad. Not every day will be a great day, not every day will be marked by forward progress, and not every day will be easier than the last. Cut yourself a little slack. None of us are perfect . . . and we seldom stay moving in the right direction for long. Get your eyes back on God, and remind yourself that tomorrow is a chance to try again. As I Peter 5:7 says, "Cast your cares on Him, for He cares for you."

- *Time is relative.* All clocks and calendars work in the same way, but time itself is relative. You may be marking time in chemo treatments, hours of sleep, or by any other measuring stick. Stop thinking about time and make the most of the moments you've been given.

- *Cherish others.* This should go without saying, but cherish your family, your friends, your coworkers, and your neighbors. You'll never know how much you need them until they aren't accessible to you.

- *Look for God moments.* Early on in our journey a family friend would call me once a week to ask me to share what I had seen God do that day. Without fail, each time she called my list would be long. It seemed that when I took time out to really focus on what God was doing I was able to trace His handiwork everywhere. When you see His hand in your life, be quick to thank Him for it.

- *Take care of yourself.* You can't take care of anyone else without first taking care of yourself. Think about the emergency procedures on a commercial airline. If you lose cabin pressure and the oxygen masks drop from the overhead compartments, what do you do? You put on your mask before you help others. What good are you if you are passed out from a lack of oxygen? Exactly my point. You must take care of yourself physically, mentally, and spiritually or you are of no use to anyone.

- *Pray without ceasing.* I finally understand what it means to have an attitude of prayer, one that keeps an open line of communication between myself and God. You really can pray about anything, anywhere.

- *Read the book.* Got concerns, fears, doubts, anxiety, and uncertainty? God has answers. BUT . . . His word can't change our hearts if we aren't reading it. It can't change our thoughts and actions if we aren't soaking it in and living it out. The pastor of my teen years was always quick to point out this truth to me. No matter what question I posed, he would always say, "Read the book." I can honestly say that has been the best advice anyone has ever given me. Not only does God have answers, He is THE ANSWER.

. . . Dig into God's Word . . .

All Scripture is God-breathed and is useful for
teaching, rebuking, correcting and training in righteousness, so
that the servant of God may be thoroughly equipped for every
good work.

- 2 Timothy 3:16-17

. . . Think, Pray, Grow . . .

Honestly evaluate your faithfulness to study God's Word.
What can you do to develop a consistent pattern of study?

_____

_____

_____

_____

Studying the Bible is a great place to start, but obedience to
the Bible is the way to live. How are you being obedient to
what you learn as you study the Bible?

_____

_____

_____

_____

And Then There Were Four

More than four years have passed since Josh's surgery to remove the remainder of his cancer, and I can't help but reflect on these last few years with wonder. As I look back, I am in wonder at how we didn't see the signs of approaching disaster, wonder at how quickly our lives and perspectives changed, wonder at how people supported us on this journey, wonder at how many miracles we have seen God do, wonder at how far Josh has come since that diagnosis, and wonder at how very much God has taught me about what it means to truly trust Him.

When I think about how we didn't see the signs of approaching disaster, I realize that we can all become blind to small changes in our lives. We can start to accept little things as normal, even if those little things are not pleasing to God. When we let those little things go unchecked, they fester into something just as dangerous and deadly as Josh's cancer.

When I think about how quickly our lives and perspectives changed, it makes me think about God's sovereignty and timing. When we were thrust so quickly into the middle of the storm, God was still in control. He still had a plan. He still loved us. He was strengthening us in the fire. He was teaching us what it really means to trust Him. My point is this: without this journey I may have never learned these truths. We can read the Bible and see how God delivered people, healed people, protected people, and led people; however, reading and experiencing are two very different things. We all know experience is the best teacher. Trust God . . . even when it is hard and you don't understand. He is trustworthy.

When I think about how many people pulled alongside us, supporting us with prayers, visits, and serving us in so many ways, I marvel at this forever family God is continuing to create. Believers are a true family . . . and it can be seen in our love for one another. So . . . keep loving each other!

When I think of the miracles I have seen God do, I am simply in awe. I want to be very clear here . . . God undeniably worked a miracle in saving Josh's life and curing him from cancer, but there are so many more miracles that are unseen. The peace I experienced is a miracle. The nights I was able to sleep "in the boat" are a miracle. The understanding God gave me (when I don't have a science bone in my body) is a miracle. The patience God is growing in me is a miracle. Miracles don't have to be big and obvious.

God is working in the small things, too. Don't miss Him there.

When I think about how far Josh has come since this journey began, I am reminded that we are all on a journey of sanctification. Just like Josh has experienced, sometimes we move forward and sometimes we slip backward. What is important is growth over time. Do your best to faithfully serve and love God, but be quick to seek His forgiveness and restoration when you go backward. Then, get back on the path of moving forward. Will it be easy? Probably not, but it will be worth it.

When I think about what it means to really trust God, I am reminded that He is still teaching me to trust Him. He is teaching us all the same thing. I marvel at how quickly I can find myself not trusting Him and worrying instead. I know I'm not alone in this. The truth is we not only can trust Him, but we must trust Him. When worries and concerns arise, we can choose to trust Him.

These last few years have been the hardest of my life, but I would not trade them for anything. I know that sounds crazy, but what God has taught me is worth more than all the struggles and pain of this season. You see, God is doing a great work in me – where He is growing my faith, strengthening my dependence on Him, producing fruit in my life – because He is teaching me how to bloom in the dark.

. . . Dig into God's Word . . .

We continually ask God to fill you with the knowledge of his will through all the wisdom and understanding that the Spirit gives, so that you may live a life worthy of the Lord and please him in every way: bearing fruit in every good work, growing in the knowledge of God, being strengthened with all power according to his glorious might so that you may have great endurance and patience, and giving joyful thanks to the Father, who has qualified you to share in the inheritance of his holy people in the kingdom of light.

– Colossians 1:9b-12

. . . Think, Pray, Grow . . .

Consider the ways you can bloom – live out what you've learned – as a result of this study. Then, write a prayer thanking God for what He is doing in your life.

_____

_____

_____

_____

_____

_____

_____

_____

~ Bibliography ~

Abad, C, et al. "Adverse Effects of Isolation in Hospitalised Patients: A Systematic Review." *PubMed*, Elsevier Ltd., 2012, https://pubmed.ncbi.nlm.nih.gov/20619929.

Berkowitz, David. "New Logo Features Strike Through Cancer." *Www.mdanderson.org*, MD Anderson Cancer Center, 2021, https://www.mdanderson.org/pubications/conquest/making-cancer-history-.h37-1585890.html.

"Chemo Brain." *Mayo Clinic*, Mayo Foundation for Medical Education and Research, 9 Feb. 2023, https://www.mayoclinic.org/diseases-conditions/chemo-brain/symptoms-causes/syc-20351060.

"Drugs: How Chemotherapy Works." *American Childhood Cancer Organization*, https://www.acco.org/drugs-how-chemotherapy-works.

Holy Bible New International Version. Zondervan, 2005.

"Matthew West Lyrics." *AZLyrics*, 2000, https://b.azlyrics.com/?u=%2Flyrics%2Fmatthewwest%2Fstrongenough.html.

"Mediastinal Germ Cell Tumours." *Cancer Research UK*, 21 Feb. 2023, https://www.cancerresearchuk.org/about-cancer/mediastinal-germ-cell-tumours.

Merville, Scott. "Immunotherapy Innovator Jim Allison's Nobel Purpose." *Www.mdanderson.org*, MD Anderson Cancer Center, 2018, https://www.mdanderson.org/publications/conquest/immunotherapy-innovator-jim-allisons-nobel-purpose.h36-1592202.html.

"Support for Caregivers of Cancer Patients." *www.cancer.gov*, National Cancer Institute, 6 Aug. 2020.

"Unspoken Lyrics." *"Tomorrow" Lyrics*, AZLyrics.com, 2000, https://www.azlyrics.com/lyrics/unspoken/tomorrow.html.

~ About the Author ~

Melissa lives in rural central Louisiana with her husband of nearly thirty years and is the mom of two adult sons. Together she and her husband Stacy are adjusting to their empty nest and enjoying spending time with their two yard dogs, gathering eggs from their backyard chickens, and working in their small business. She is a Christ follower who loves serving as a Bible study teacher and pianist in her local church.

Made in United States
North Haven, CT
23 July 2024

55348217R10070